To Auguste, for his First Communion.
B. G.

Under the direction of Romain Lizé, Vice President, MAGNIFICAT

Editor, MAGNIFICAT: Isabelle Galmiche
Editor, Ignatius: Vivian Dudro
Assistant of the Editor: Pascale Vandewalle
Layout Designers: Élise Borel, Jean-Marc Richard
Proofreader: Cameron Pollette
Production: Thierry Dubus, Sabine Marioni

Original French edition:
Pierre, apôtre de Jesus
© 2008 by Groupe Fleurus, Paris
© 2014 by MAGNIFICAT Inc., New York • Ignatius Press, San Francisco
All rights reserved
ISBN Ignatius Press 978-1-58617-922-9
ISBN MAGNIFICAT 978-1-936260-83-6
The trademark MAGNIFICAT depicted in this publication is used under license from and is the exclusive property
of Magnificat Central Service Team, Inc., A Ministry to Catholic Women, and may not be used without its written consent.
Printed by Tien Wah Press, Malaysia
Printed on January 2014
Job Number 14001
Printed in Singapore in compliance with the Consumer Protection Safety Act, 2008.

The Life of a Saint

Peter
Apostle of Jesus

Text: Boris Grébille – Illustrations: Hervé Florès

Translated by Janet Chevrier

Ignatius   MAGNIFICAT®

The Fisherman of Galilee

"Here they come! Here they come!" Simon shouted.

The boats were coming in from the lake, and their nets were full of fish glistening in the sunshine. Simon was proud of his father: he was such a great fisherman.

When Simon grew up, he would be a fisherman too.

"What a bad catch today!" said Simon.

He and his brother Andrew frowned at their empty net.

From the shore, a man shouted to them, "Go out deeper and cast your net again!"

The two brothers were surprised. Who was this man telling them what to do? But when they hauled up the net again, it was so full of fish that it was breaking!

The fishermen were amazed at the number of fish.

They trembled before the man and Simon said: "Go away from me, Lord, for I am a sinful man!"

But the man replied to him: "Do not be afraid. I am Jesus. Come, follow me. From now on, you will be fishers of men!"

Simon and his brother left their boats and followed Jesus.

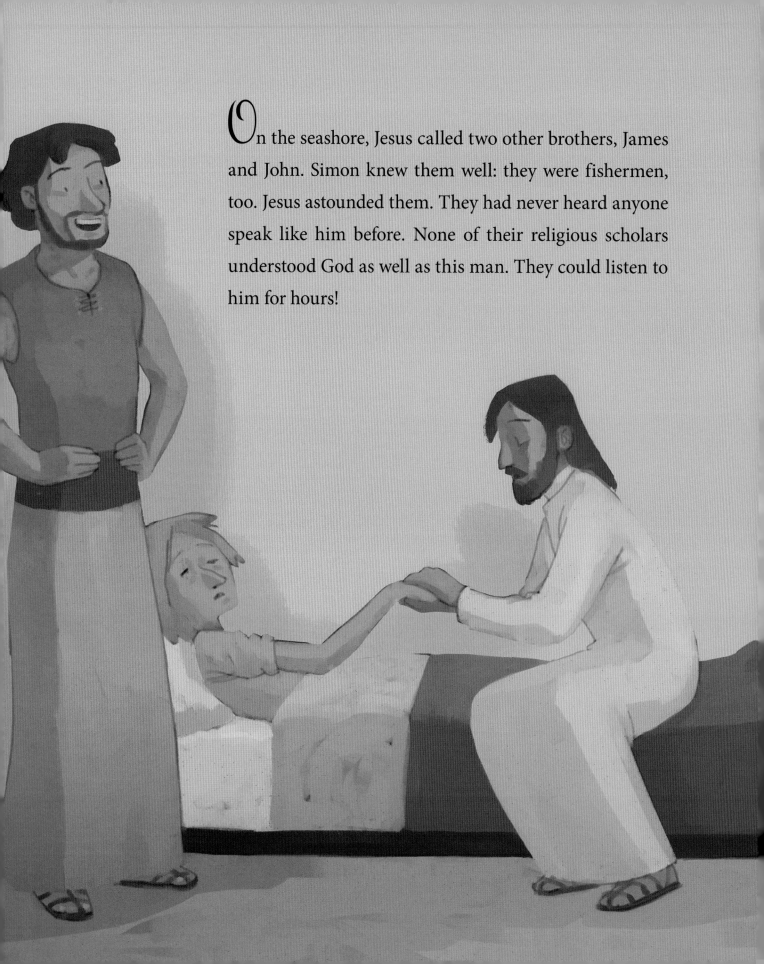

On the seashore, Jesus called two other brothers, James and John. Simon knew them well: they were fishermen, too. Jesus astounded them. They had never heard anyone speak like him before. None of their religious scholars understood God as well as this man. They could listen to him for hours!

$\mathcal{A}$s it was getting late, Simon said to Jesus, "Come to my house for supper."

Jesus went inside, and Simon told him that his mother-in-law was sick in bed with a fever. Jesus went over to the woman, took her by the hand, and gently lifted her up. Immediately, she was cured.

The whole house rejoiced. Simon looked at Jesus with amazement: this man would change his life!

By now, Jesus had twelve special friends, the Apostles.

As they were crossing the lake, Simon was thinking of all the wonders he had seen Jesus do. That very day, Jesus had fed a huge crowd with only five loaves of bread and two fish! And there were leftovers!

Suddenly, one of the Twelve cried out, "Look, a ghost!"

But it was Jesus, walking on the water. Without hesitation, Simon asked Jesus to call him. He climbed out of the boat and walked on the water. Then, all at once, Simon became frightened and began to sink. "Lord, save me!" he cried. Jesus reached out his hand and grabbed Simon.

"Why did you doubt?" he asked with a smile.

The Twelve traveled through the countryside with Jesus. Sometimes Jesus sent them out two by two to proclaim the mercy of God and to heal the sick. Simon was happy with this new life of his. Truly he had become a fisher of men.

One day, Jesus asked the Twelve, "When people talk about me, who do they say that I am?"

"They say you are a prophet."

"And, you, who do you say that I am?"

Simon answered, "You are the Christ, the Son of the living God."

Jesus looked at Simon and said, "Blessed are you, for God has taught you this. You are Peter, and on this rock I will build my Church. I will give you the keys to my kingdom."

Peter was very proud of his new name, which means "rock".

The Apostle of Jesus

Jesus brought Peter, James, and John to a mountaintop. Suddenly, the face of Jesus shone like the sun, and his clothing became dazzling white. Two men, Moses and Elijah, appeared on either side of him. Then the voice of God thundered, "This is my beloved Son; listen to him!"

And Peter, James, and John fell to the ground in awe.

Many people did not believe Jesus was the Son of God. As time went by, they wished to put him to death.

Jesus and his Apostles arrived in Jerusalem. Before the Last Supper, Jesus took a basin of water and began washing the feet of his friends.

$\mathcal{P}$eter objected: "Master, you will never wash my feet!"

"If I don't, you cannot come with me."

"In that case, wash my hands and my head, too!"

"No, you are clean. I am giving you this as an example, that you in turn should wash the feet of those whom you will serve in my name."

During supper, Jesus announced that one of the twelve Apostles would betray him. One of the disciples asked him, "Which one of us will betray you?"

Jesus replied, "The one to whom I give this food will turn me in." With that, Jesus handed a morsel of food to Judas, saying to him, "Go: do what you have to do."

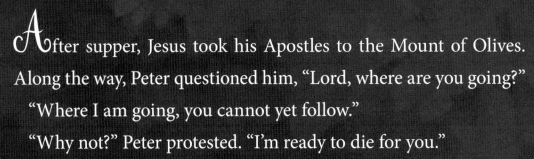

After supper, Jesus took his Apostles to the Mount of Olives. Along the way, Peter questioned him, "Lord, where are you going?"

"Where I am going, you cannot yet follow."

"Why not?" Peter protested. "I'm ready to die for you."

Then Jesus said, "Are you, Peter? Before the cock crows twice, you will deny me three times."

$\mathcal{P}$eter was hurt. How could Jesus think such a thing of him?

When they arrived in the garden, Jesus asked Peter, James, and John to stay a little way off and to keep watch while he prayed. But the three friends fell asleep. When Jesus woke them, they saw some guards arriving with Judas.

They had come to arrest Jesus. Peter wanted to defend his Master with his sword, but Jesus stopped him and gave himself up.

As the guards took Jesus to be questioned, all the disciples except Peter became afraid and ran away. From a distance, Peter followed after Jesus and entered the high priest's courtyard. As he warmed himself by a fire, a maid said, "You were with Jesus."

"I do not know what you mean", Peter replied.

He went to the porch, where another woman said, "This man was with Jesus."

Again Peter denied it: "No, I was not."

Then some others said to Peter, "Certainly you are one of Jesus' friends."

Peter was frightened and said, "No, I do not know the man!"

Just then the cock crowed for the second time. Remembering what Jesus had said, Peter wept in shame and sorrow.

*P*eter was very sad. Jesus had been crucified. He had died, and his body had been buried. Peter and John wondered what would become of them. Suddenly, Mary Magdalen rushed in, out of breath. "Jesus has disappeared!" she cried. "His body is gone!"

*P*eter and John hurried out. They ran all the way to the tomb. The heavy stone blocking the entrance had been rolled aside. They entered the tomb and saw that it was empty. The cloth Jesus' body had been wrapped in was folded up. Then they remembered something Jesus had said: "After three days, I will rise again."

The disciples went home but Mary Magdalene stayed at the tomb. Jesus appeared to her there. She returned to the disciples and exclaimed, "Jesus is alive! I have seen the risen Lord!"

The Head of the Church

Peter and his friends had not caught a single fish! From the shore, a man called out, "Cast the net again!" They did so, and soon the net was bursting with fish.

Peter understood: the man was the risen Christ. He jumped into the water and swam over to him. All together, they ate the fish and bread. Three times Jesus asked, "Do you love me?" And three times Peter said yes. "You will be the shepherd of my sheep", Jesus told him.

Before Jesus returned to his Father in heaven, he gathered his Apostles and told them to teach and to baptize everyone. He promised to send the Holy Spirit to help them.

One day, as they were praying in a house in Jerusalem, a sound like that of a great wind rushed into the room; what looked like flames rested upon their heads, and with that, they were all filled with the Holy Spirit. With new confidence, they spoke about God in many different languages.

Some said, "They've had too much to drink!" Others thought, "It's a miracle!"

A crowd gathered outside the house, and Peter addressed them: "My friends, Jesus, whom you crucified, has been raised from the dead. We are witnesses of this. Jesus is alive, and today he has sent us the Holy Spirit."

"What should we do?" the people asked.

"Reform your lives, every one of you, and be baptized. It was for you that Jesus came among us."

That day, the Apostles baptized three thousand people!

Peter was happy: more and more people believed in Jesus.

One day, when he was with John, a beggar stopped them. Paralyzed since birth, this man had never been able to walk.

"I have no money," said Peter, "but I will give you an even greater treasure: in the name of Jesus Christ, stand up and walk!"

And the man immediately got up and walked!

The crowd shouted with joy, giving thanks to God. But some men were furious: they had gotten rid of Jesus, but now his friends were attracting everyone's attention!

Peter traveled all over the region around Jerusalem. He healed the sick, he baptized, and he celebrated the breaking of the bread as Jesus had instructed.

Cornelius, a centurion in the Roman army, sent for Peter. He told Peter that he had been visited by an angel. Unlike Jesus and his Apostles, Cornelius was not a Jew, but he loved God and his neighbor.

As Peter listened to Cornelius, he understood: Jesus had come not only for the Jews, but for the whole world. Peter baptized Cornelius and everyone in his household. He then told the other Apostles that they must share the good news of God's love and mercy with all the peoples of the earth.

*L*ife in Jerusalem was hard for those who believed in Jesus. King Herod did not like them. He put Peter and other Christians in prison. Some he even killed.

*P*eter left Jerusalem and eventually settled in Rome. He led the Christians there the way he guided the whole Church. He wrote important letters to the faithful in other cities.

The Roman government also turned against the Christians and had many arrested and killed. Peter too was killed. He was crucified upside down.

$\mathcal{S}$imon, the fisherman, became Peter, Apostle of Jesus Christ. As the chief shepherd of the flock, Peter was the first pope.

Over his tomb in Rome is an immense and beautiful church that bears his name. Every day, thousands of pilgrims from around the world go there to pray and to remember this friend of Jesus.

Feast Days

Saint Peter is commemorated several times during the year:
• June 29, on the same day as Saint Paul
• February 22, on the feast of the Chair of Saint Peter
• November 18, on the feast of the Dedication of the Basilicas of Saints Peter and Paul

The First Pope

Jesus chose Peter to be the head of the Church, that is, the first pope.
Francis, who was elected when Benedict XVI retired in 2013,
is the 266th pope of the Catholic Church.
The pope is elected by the cardinals during a meeting called a conclave.
It can last several days, but the cardinals are not allowed to leave during
the conclave because the details of the election must remain secret.

Saint Peter's Basilica

The first basilica was built by Constantine I, the first Christian Roman emperor,
over the site where Saint Peter was buried. The new basilica was built in the sixteenth century.
Construction lasted more than a hundred years, and great artists, such as Michelangelo,
contributed to this gigantic and gorgeous church.

The Keys of Saint Peter

Saint Peter is often depicted holding keys, which can also be seen on the papal coat of arms,
or crest, because of these words spoken by Jesus himself: "I will give you the keys
of the kingdom of heaven, and whatever you bind on earth shall be bound in heaven,
and whatever you loose on earth shall be loosed in heaven" (Mt 16:19).